T0194220

And There I Was

Agatha Patane

iUniverse, Inc.
Bloomington

And There I Was

Copyright © 2011 by Agatha Patane

All rights reserved. No part of this book may be used or reproduced by any means, graphic, electronic, or mechanical, including photocopying, recording, taping or by any information storage retrieval system without the written permission of the publisher except in the case of brief quotations embodied in critical articles and reviews.

The views expressed in this work are solely those of the author and do not necessarily reflect the views of the publisher, and the publisher hereby disclaims any responsibility for them.

iUniverse books may be ordered through booksellers or by contacting:

iUniverse
1663 Liberty Drive
Bloomington, IN 47403
www.iuniverse.com
1-800-Authors (1-800-288-4677)

Because of the dynamic nature of the Internet, any web addresses or links contained in this book may have changed since publication and may no longer be valid.

Any people depicted in stock imagery provided by Thinkstock are models, and such images are being used for illustrative purposes only.

Certain stock imagery © Thinkstock.

ISBN: 978-1-4502-9568-0 (sc)
ISBN: 978-1-4502-9569-7 (hc)
ISBN: 978-1-4502-9570-3 (ebk)

Printed in the United States of America

iUniverse rev. date: 07/22/2011

Dedicated to Joe Kita for the inspiration to write this memoir

Contents

Chapter 1

America, Part 1

Yes, I was a Lady Marine. I was so proud.

I wanted to be my own person, free of any bonds. I told my mother I was going to join the United States Marine Corps. And so I did, in 1943, as part of the first round of Lady Marines.

Our unit trained at Hunter College in New York for several months. We studied all the names of the VIPs in Washington DC and in the Marine Corps. We learned the ranks of personnel and the names of the generals in the Marine Corps, Army, and Air Force. We had so much to learn before we were transferred to Marine Corps Headquarters just outside of Washington DC.

The first Lady Marines lived at Henderson Hall in Arlington, Virginia. Our first mission after we received our uniforms was to march proudly in a parade, wearing them. The uniforms were beautiful—green with bright red scarves and a green cap with a red tassel. At the parade, First Lady Mrs. Roosevelt honored us from the viewing stand. I still have that photograph of Mrs. Roosevelt. It was a great day for the Marines.

Marine Headquarters was amazing. Memorizing the ranks of the Marines was one of our jobs—and we had to know each one's rank. It seemed I was forever saluting. I loved Washington, and I loved the Marine Corps. Life was beautiful. I settled into my secretarial position and met so many Marines. There was one I remember distinctly—he was a major, so elegant and with so much personality. I loved his stories and his humor. He was later transferred overseas.

Marine Corps Ball, Washington, D.C.,

Our pay was $54 a month, which, even considering the times, was not very much. That money had to cover the cost of dry-cleaning our uniforms, laundry, cosmetics, toothpaste, and many other necessities. At the end of the month, most of us were without funds. One day several of the girls decided to take a bus trip from Arlington to Washington to go window-shopping. The bus fare was ten cents each way. I had twenty cents left for the month. One of the girls wanted to go with us but she didn't have any money, so I gave her the ten cents for the bus to town. When it was time to return to Arlington, I realized I had given her my last dime. I had no choice but to walk back to Henderson Hall. It was several hours before I arrived—so tired, but so happy to return home safely.

After a year at headquarters, I met a Marine captain named Jerry. He was handsome and a bit older. We dated occasionally and became good friends. His time in the Marine Corps was coming to an end, and he had decided to finish his education under the GI Bill of Rights. He enrolled at Catholic University in Washington to pursue his PhD. Jerry worked on his PhD dissertation for two years, and I helped him as much as I could—typing and retyping his work for him; there were always changes and more changes. Finally, he finished his dissertation and received his doctorate. He later accepted a position at the University of Detroit. Throughout the whole experience, he became the love of my life.

I received my honorable discharge from the Marine Corps two-and-a-half years later in 1945, but continued to work at the headquarters as a civilian. I also continued my education under the GI Bill of Rights, studying French, Spanish, and German at the Berlitz School of Languages. At Christmastime, I flew to Detroit to meet Jerry's family. At that time he gave me an engagement ring; we made plans to be married in the spring.

I left Detroit in the clouds, with many wonderful thoughts of how our life together would be. We talked on the phone for hours on end throughout the following six months. One day he mentioned he would be driving to Washington on New Year's Eve. I waited and waited for his arrival. I was so worried there had been an accident that I finally called his sister in Detroit. She seemed very sad when she informed me that he had married one of his students and was on his way to Washington to accept a position at a university. I was devastated. What happened? There was never an explanation or an apology. Jerry just disappeared from my life.

One day I was walking in Washington, and I spotted him walking toward me with a young blonde. I panicked and darted across the street, because I did not want to face him and his cruelty. Cars came to a screeching halt, and I was almost killed. That was the day I decided to make a change in my life.

The next day I went to the US Air Attaché Office and asked for a position as far away from Washington as possible. They informed me that there was an opening for a social secretary in their office in Tehran, Iran. I'd never heard of Tehran, but I accepted immediately.

Chapter 2

Tehran, Iran

It wasn't until I had taken the job with the Air Attaché in Tehran that I reflected on my decision. I was giving up my job in Washington, my car, and my friends. I was headed into an unknown life. But despite the sacrifices, I was determined to honor my contract—and see the world.

It was a cold, dismal day when the plane left Westover Air Force Base in Massachusetts. The memory is still just as crisp as the brisk wind that struck me as I boarded the plane. I was leaving for a new land, and I was scared but hopeful. I was going to be secretary to the Air Attaché at the American Embassy, but my journey to Tehran was not as straightforward as my orders.

Somehow there was a mix-up and I found myself aboard a troop plane. I was sitting alongside officers—enlisted men—and I was the only girl aboard. It wasn't until we were airborne that I was informed I should have taken another plane, but at that point I had to make the best of it. We all settled down in our bucket seats, and I must say we had a jolly time. I enjoyed the trip in spite of the uncomfortable accommodations, and surprisingly, I never felt scared.

When we arrived in Germany, I checked in for the transfer but was told there would not be another plane leaving for Tehran until the following week. Arrangements were made for me to stay at a military hotel in the interim. Because it was my first time outside the United States, I decided to make the most of it. I rented a car and explored the area. I was quite impressed with the friendliness of the Germans; they were so kind and helpful everywhere I traveled.

A week later, happy—and a bit stuffed from all the wonderful whipped-cream pastries I had indulged in—I boarded a Pan American flight to Tehran. I sat with a young nurse from the World Health Organization, who lived in Tehran. We passed the time talking, and she told me she knew of a party planned in Tehran a few days after we arrived; then she asked if I would like to attend and meet her friends. I was so happy to have met someone, I immediately accepted.

Finally, after a long flight, we reached Iran. As the plane descended, I looked out the window and saw mountains of sand. It was hot, dusty, and barren. Fear struck me. Loneliness set in. What had I done? What was I doing here?

Fortunately, two gentlemen from the Air Attaché office were waiting to meet me at the landing strip. I was overjoyed to see them. They took care of my luggage as well as all the details of entering a foreign country. They took me for a quick tour of the city—that was when the reality of the country started to set in. I actually saw men hanging in the square for crimes they had committed. I felt terrible and looked the other way. My escorts informed me that a Pan American plane had crashed into a mountain the week before, killing several Air Attaché personnel.

Ferdozi Square, Teheran

After this sobering introduction to the city, the men drove me to a small hotel close to the American Embassy where I would stay until I found an apartment. The next morning they picked me up and took me to the office. I was welcomed aboard; everyone was so friendly that my fear left me. I was introduced to the attaché personnel and then initiated into my job. My duties included answering invitations (some in French; my Berlitz kicked in) and informing the Attaché of the parties he was to attend, as well as the dress code of the evening.

I was fortunate to find a four-room apartment in a bright yellow, three-story building close to the embassy. I lived on the second floor. My friends picked me up and drove me to the office every day even though I was only a few blocks away. There were many military and foreign functions each week and sometimes several in one evening.

I was fortunate to attend quite a few of these. It soon became my way of life, and I enjoyed all the attaché personnel and their families. I also attended many World Health Organization events through my friendship with the nurse I had met on the plane. But living in Tehran wasn't all glitz and glamour.

Running water was scarce in Tehran. People gathered at *jubes*—areas with running water on both sides of the street—to brush their teeth, bathe, and do laundry. Today, *jubes* no longer exist; Tehran is a modern city with hotels, restaurants, and department stores.

I witnessed many religious rituals in Tehran. One was a parade where men marched down the street bare-chested, beating themselves with chains until they bled. When they marched, no one else was allowed on the streets. One day I peeked out the window of my apartment while they were marching, petrified that I'd be seen. All of the men did an about-face and looked in my direction but fortunately kept marching. I later learned that just a few blocks away an American newsman was killed for trying to photograph the event.

I later discovered the significance of the ritual, which is practiced as part of the observance of Muharram, according to Mr. Salah at the American Embassy in Tehran. During this period of deep mourning, some men self-flagellate in order to experience grief and pain firsthand.

About a year into my time in Tehran, I took a trip to Geneva, Switzerland. There were nine of us from the office, plus the secretary to the Ambassador of Tehran. I really didn't have many duties to fulfill, so I decided to travel as much as possible. My friend had business in Rome, so I went to meet her for dinner at a restaurant. She ordered in Italian for both of us. Soon a beautiful dish of "I don't know" was placed in front of me. I asked her what it was and she said, "Octopus, it's delicious." There are many things I will not eat today—one of them is octopus.

I stayed in Rome for several days and visited the Trevi Fountain and St. Peter's. My friend had gone on to Taormina, Sicily, and I met her there a few days later. I rented a Fiat and drove to the castle where she was staying, and we toured many parts of the island together. Taormina was a beautiful seaside resort town where, I later learned, Winston Churchill vacationed.

I flew back to Rome, stayed at the Savoy Hotel for a few days, and then flew to Paris. I met up with some friends from Washington and we went shopping together. My former superior from Washington was stationed at the American Embassy. He and his wife took me out for dinner (no octopus), and I had a wonderful evening. The next day I called another friend who was at the American Embassy, and she suggested we go to the horse races with some more friends. She picked me up at the hotel, and we had a marvelous day. Even though I didn't know what I was doing, I won five thousand francs in the last race.

My next stop was Brussels, Belgium, where I visited more old friends from Washington. They lived outside Brussels, so I had to take a train. I stayed for two days and then went to London to do a little shopping.

Finally, it was time to return to Geneva and eventually Tehran. After all the adventure, it was good to return to work and settle into a routine again. Little did I know that my life was about to change dramatically.

At a work function, I met an attaché from the army office, named Dave. He was young, handsome, and we instantly liked each other. I dated him occasionally when I was off duty, and in less than a year we became engaged. We were at a party, and when we left he gave me a little box with a diamond ring in it. We were married at a small French Catholic church in Tehran on October 9, 1955. The Air Attaché gave me away. My bridesmaid was the young nurse from World Health. And the Air Attaché and his wife hosted the reception at their magnificent home. I was beginning another new life.

Dave and I settled into a new home with the sweetest and most efficient maid, named Fatima. She wore a *shedora*, a dress that covered her whole body and head except for her eyes. After arriving at our house for work at 6:00 a.m., she'd remove it, and she was very pretty. She did everything for us except cook. I did that, mostly breakfast.

Our home in Teheran

One day, friends from the American Embassy visited with their four-year-old daughter, who spoke fluent Farsi. Since we were going out, we asked the little girl to tell Fatima that she could leave. She went into the kitchen and said (in Farsi), "You are finished. Get out." Fatima came in crying. We had to console her that she wasn't finished—she could simply go home for the evening.

There were adventures outside the home, too. One evening, Dave and I were invited to the palace where the Shah of Iran lived with his wife, Empress Soraya. I'll never forget her descending the staircase, regal and beautiful, wearing a white gown with one shoulder bare. She was the most elegant lady I have ever seen in my life.

During another event—an Iranian dinner we attended with the Air Attaché—goats' eyes were served on a beautiful platter to the guest of honor. The guest of honor that evening was the Air Attaché's wife. She looked at the eyes and said to me, "I can't." But all the guests were waiting for her and would have been insulted had she not tasted the honorary dish. So she gulped them down, excused herself from the table, and threw up in the ladies' room. Luckily, I was never a guest of honor.

The Attaché and the embassy offices occasionally held formal evening functions outdoors. I remember the grounds were covered with beautiful, plush Persian rugs that were delightful to walk on. (I later found that the Persians clean their rugs by laying them out on the streets and letting cars drive over them.)

One evening, the Harlem Globetrotters basketball team visited Tehran. Although I am not a sports fan, Dave was, and he purchased tickets. He was very happy to watch the game, but we sat for hours on a hard bench in the heat. For some reason, they weren't selling water, soda, or any liquids. When it was over, we immediately drove home, and Dave fixed us both a Scotch and water. When he handed it to me, I drank it in one gulp; it was without a doubt the thirstiest I had ever been. Dave asked why I drank it so fast—did I think it was water?

Life in Tehran wasn't all play. There was plenty of work to be done, although we were generally in the office only from 8:00 a.m. to 1:00 p.m. on weekdays, with weekends and holidays off. We took many trips, visiting the surrounding cities and countries. We flew to Isfahan, Iran's second-largest city, for a week. We took a small Iranian Air plane, which held about six people. It shook and swayed all the way, and I thought it would crash at any moment. But we arrived safely and checked into the only hotel in town.

Dave and I visited many other exotic places as well. We went to the Taj Mahal in India at a time when very few tourists went there. We flew to Cairo and rode the camels at the pyramids. It cost only three or four dollars to mount the camel, but what the guides didn't tell you was that when you wanted to dismount, you had to pay again. While we were in Egypt we also visited Luxor and the Valley of the Kings. We walked many steps down into the tombs, but when we began the climb back out there seemed to be many more. Even though I was young, I was exhausted by the time we reached the exit. I remember a little boy selling Coca-Cola at a stand. It was the coolest Coke I have ever had in my life.

We also loved beautiful Beirut, Lebanon, which we visited several times. The shopping was fantastic. I bought a dozen beaded evening purses every time I visited and gave them to my friends. I paid about two dollars for each one, and today they cost hundreds of dollars. If only I had one today! Beirut has been demolished many, many times since—and has been rebuilt again and again.

Travel wasn't always for fun, though. Because we lived so far from the United States, sometimes we had to fly for necessity. My father had a stroke while I was living in Tehran. My mother wired me to return home because she didn't think he would survive. It took me three days before I finally arrived in Pennsylvania.

The trip was stressful and hectic, but my father survived, and I returned to Tehran.

For Christmas one year, Dave gave me a small Fiat with a big red bow. I was delighted, and drove it everywhere. But that Fiat wasn't my greatest gift. That December I also became pregnant. I was healthy, happy, and looked wonderful.

Because Dave's two-year tour of duty in Tehran was coming to an end, and because children born within the country of Iran are considered Iranian regardless of their parents' heritage, we contacted Washington and asked for a transfer to Europe. Soon, we received orders to report to the American Embassy in Athens, Greece. When we left, we sold my Fiat to an Iranian. He did not have a license, but he was so happy to have a car. We watched him drive away at seventy mph.

Chapter 3

Athens, Greece

Our plane left Tehran early in the morning, and when we arrived in Athens, we checked into the Palace Hotel. To start the day off right, I decided to go to the beauty shop to have my hair done, while Dave called for a car to check in at the American Embassy. Here I thought we were going to have a normal afternoon settling into our new country.

But while I was at the hairdresser I heard shouting and yelling in the streets. I asked what was going on, and the hairdresser said it was a riot! Dave came rushing in and told me we had to get back to the hotel immediately. He left money at the desk, and we rushed out.

The doors and windows of the hotel were being boarded up, and only registered guests could enter. They ushered us in, and we went to our room. But we were soon told that an embassy car was waiting outside for Dave. When he walked out the door I grabbed my camera and looked out the window. I saw the car at the entrance and Dave rushing toward it. Then the rioters rushed the car. They swarmed all over it, lifted it into the air, and eventually overturned it. I couldn't believe what I was seeing! But then I saw Dave scrambling out and running back to the hotel. My camera was capturing all the action. To this day I don't know what the rioting was about, but it lasted for three days. Luckily, the driver escaped as well.

After the chaos of our first days in Athens died down, we started looking for a place to live—ideally, far from the bustling downtown. Greece is a fascinating country with picturesque ruins, beautiful scenery, and unique customs, so it was fun to explore. We ended up renting a beautifully landscaped house close to the white-sand beaches of Glyfada, south of Athens. We were the only Americans in the neighborhood, and I was very lonely. No one, including our maid, spoke English, and I had yet to make any friends. By this time I was also six months pregnant.

Since there were no American hospitals in Athens, I went to the American Embassy dispensary for a checkup. But after examining me, the two young doctors said I wasn't pregnant. Instead, they said, it was a tumor, but they put me on a cot and proceeded to conduct a battery of tests. Later, they sent me home.

The following day I was supposed to meet Dave in Athens to shop for window curtains. His friend was supposed to pick me up and drive me there. When his friend arrived I was so sick I asked him to call Dave and tell him I couldn't make it. My husband came home and he called the dispensary. The hospital told him to bring me in immediately. The doctors put me in a bed, gave me a laxative, and told me to relax. The next thing I remember was a nurse standing over me. Then a doctor appeared, who told me that I had lost twins—a boy and a girl.

It was the greatest tragedy of my life. I remained at the dispensary for a few days and was then transferred to a hospital in Tripoli, where I stayed for a few more days before finally returning home. I was still very ill and the same young doctors who had diagnosed my twins as a tumor now recommended that I have a hysterectomy. They sent me to the American Hospital in Wiesbaden, Germany. I went alone; Dave was working, but would come the next day.

When I arrived in Wiesbaden, the doctors examined me and scheduled the operation for the next afternoon. In the morning I took a walk around the hospital and prayed and came to a decision: I wasn't going to have the operation. I flew back to Athens via military air and had someone from the embassy meet me at the airport to drive me home. When I walked in the door, Dave was shocked. He had been planning to fly to Germany in just a few hours. I told him I had decided against the surgery.

An elderly nurse at the dispensary heard what had happened to me and suggested I contact Dr. Pierre Cattaneo in Rome. He was a highly respected physician and professor, and I was blessed to get an appointment with him. Dave and I flew to Rome the following week and took a taxi to his office. He turned out to be the sweetest, kindest doctor I have ever met in my life. He examined me and said I was fine and would be able to have children. He even suggested that we transfer to Rome so that I could be under his care.

Dave and I flew back to Athens, greatly relieved. After all we'd been through, we decided to give up our house in Glyfada and move closer to the embassy, where I could make more friends and not feel so secluded. We found an apartment in a high-rise about a mile from the office. I loved this apartment and soon found a friend in the building. Her name was Irene, and she suggested I study Greek; so every morning I started driving to classes at the embassy.

Irene had a four-year-old son, whom she would bring with her whenever she visited. One evening Dave was working on a project that required his total concentration, but Irene's son was running through the apartment making noise. Dave finally asked Irene to leave and take her son with her. Irene was very upset, and I was furious with Dave. She was the only friend I had in the building, and Athens had not proven to be as social as Tehran.

If there's one thing that I remember about the Greeks, it's that they're much more boisterous than people in other countries. They love to cook, drink, and party—and they don't start until late. A typical evening commenced at 8:00 or 9:00 p.m. One night, Irene had a formal party for fifty guests in her apartment. She asked me to keep her company while she was cooking. When I arrived, there was a large pig's head boiling in a pot on the stove along with many other unusual dishes. The guests arrived dressed in evening clothes and enjoyed a great buffet dinner. Everyone drank retsina wine, which tasted like kerosene to me. Dave and I had a good time, but we were happy to return to our apartment for a Scotch and water.

We also traveled to the Greek Islands. They were magnificent, but no one spoke English at that time. One day I went on a tour with a group of ladies. One woman needed to find a restroom, but no one could understand her. I went into a restaurant and spoke Greek to explain things to the waiter. *"Pou ine tomeras?"* He quickly escorted her to the restroom. My Greek lessons were paying off.

I was becoming better at making friends, too. During our stay in Athens, we met Yargos (George) and his wife through mutual friends in Washington. We socialized with them quite often and met many of their friends. Yargos was in the clothing business. He and his wife loved to eat, drink, and dance until the wee hours of the morning. I learned a Greek dance that I still love to this day. Our social circle was finally expanding.

I continued my Greek lessons at the embassy. Despite it being one of the most difficult languages I had ever studied, I was soon able to read, write, and speak it fairly well. One day while Yargos was visiting, he asked why I had a Greek newspaper on the table. When I picked it up and read the headlines, he was shocked.

Soon, however, our two-year assignment in Athens started to wind down. Dave received his new orders: Rome, Italy. We were in the clouds.

Chapter 4

Rome, Italy

It was a wonderful feeling to leave Athens after so much tragedy. Our plane landed in Rome, and attaché personnel drove us to a hotel where we would stay until we found suitable quarters. In just a few weeks, we were fortunate to find a beautiful apartment, rented to us by a doctor who had bought and furnished it for his daughter. She had become engaged to a man in the United States and, much to the devastation of her father, would not be returning. The doctor was such a sweet person. He was overjoyed that we loved the apartment so much. There was a living room with beautiful drapes and red and black furniture. The bathroom was beige with brown marble and a square tub with indirect lighting. The floors in the apartment were all white marble. It also had a modern kitchen with all the necessary appliances as well as glass counters and shelves. There were two bedrooms and a servant's room with a separate entrance. A balcony encircled the whole apartment with stairs leading to a beautiful garden, which had flowers everywhere, and a pond with goldfish. There was also a lovely patio with benches and tables. An enclosed room off the patio could serve as a garage (although we did not have a car yet) or as a room for entertaining.

Eventually, though, Dave bought a silver Alfa Romeo for me and a Chevy for himself from an officer at the embassy who was leaving for the States. We parked both cars on the street. We had the Alfa Romeo for a few days when one night we heard a roar outside. By the time we looked out the window, it was gone. I called the police and, in very limited Italian, tried to explain what happened: "Now a car and now no car." The policeman laughed and said: "Stolen."

The Alfa Romeo was found a few days later. It was used for a robbery, and it was filthy. Fortunately, our insurance company cleaned and repaired it. Little did we know this would not be the last time we would go through this ordeal. The same car was stolen eight times in the five years we lived in Rome. It was always found and returned to us by the police. When we left the country we tried to sell it. The Italians didn't want it because it used too much gas, and the Americans didn't want it because they knew it would be stolen. We sold it to a used car dealer for a fraction of its cost.

Patio in Rome

Nonetheless, we grew to love Rome and Italy. One of my most memorable experiences occurred at a horseracing track. We were at the track one day, and in the next box sat Mario Lanza, an American tenor and movie star, along with his wife and another American actor, Dale Robertson, and his wife. We became friends. Mario told us he loved Rome so much he would like to spend the rest of his life here. He had four children, and each one had a nanny. They lived in a beautiful house in the city. Mario was preparing to film a movie at the time and was on a strict diet to lose weight for his role. During his stay at Hospital Salvator Mundi, he would sing to the patients.

To keep myself busy, I applied for a position in the embassy. They offered me a job meeting evacuees from Beirut, Lebanon, at the airport and driving them to their hotels. It would certainly have been exciting work, but since I'd have to be on 24-hour call I turned it down. I eventually took another position at the embassy.

Gina Lollabrigida
Marine Corps Ball, Rome

One day I received a call from two nuns who had been my teachers at an academy in the States. They were in Rome for a few days and wanted to visit me. (My sister had told them I lived in the city.) I picked them up at their hotel and drove them around Rome for hours. When I was in high school my father had bought me a brand new Ford for my sixteenth birthday, and I used to drive the nuns around when I was a teenager. They had a great day, plus they received the papal certificate from Pope Pius while they were there. They said they were so proud to see me living in a foreign country and doing so well.

A year after arriving in Rome, Dave and I learned that I was pregnant again. I ended up having a C-section, and I heard that Dr. Cattaneo was so proud he paraded our beautiful baby girl around the hospital. Marianne had large brown eyes and golden hair. Dr. Cattaneo and his American wife, Romana, were her godparents. To be born in Rome and baptized at St. Peter's is quite an honor. Marianne wore a long white-lace gown, and Romana carried her down the aisle on a beautiful pillow. It was quite an affair with all our friends from the embassy attending. Afterward, we had a christening party at which we gave everyone a small, beautiful silver box. It was a glorious day.

When we arrived in Rome, we had hired a maid named Maria. She was with us the entire five years we were in Rome and became like a member of the family. Maria informed me that children in Italy are potty-trained by the time they are six months old, so I dutifully purchased a potty chair for Marianne. The first time it was a disaster, but as the days went by, Marianne learned what the chair was for and started pointing to it. We couldn't believe it! She was trained in less than six months—a true Italian girl!

We did a lot of traveling with Marianne, and wherever we went her potty chair went with us. In those days they didn't have car seats, so I would hold her on my lap. If we were driving and she'd point to the chair, Dave would have to stop. We took her to Venice and for a ride on a gondola. I always dressed her like a little doll in beautiful dresses my mother sent from the States. Even though she was a baby, she seemed to enjoy every minute of our trips.

One day back at home I was listening to the radio when it was announced that Mario Lanza had died. I couldn't believe it. I remembered well what he had said about loving Rome so much he wanted to spend the rest of his life here. He was mourned in Rome and everywhere, a great voice forever stilled.

In October I became pregnant again and Dr. Cattaneo was as delighted as we were. Our beautiful son David was born by C-section in June 1960. He was such a sweet baby, with blue eyes and a mass of golden curls. Our second bedroom now contained Marianne's bed and David's crib.

Marianne & David
Baptized at St. Peter's, Rome

Soon we only had four months before our tour in Rome was over, and we decided to take another trip with the children. This time we picked Sicily. We had a great time driving the winding roads of this enchanting land, especially Taormina, a small, ancient town on the east coast of Sicily. Both of our children were wonderful travelers; even though our baby was too young to enjoy the scenery, he was content in his car-bed.

Eventually, Dave received orders that we had to return to Washington. Rome had become our home, and we were sad to leave this wonderful country and our friends. But we had no choice. Marianne was two years old, and David was just four months old. We shipped some of our furniture, put other things in storage, and packed what was necessary for our new adventure.

This time, instead of flying, we took a ship. We departed for America on a luxury liner called the SS *United States*, which was on its last voyage. It was a beautiful ship, and all the passengers just loved the children.

We stayed in touch with Dr. Cattaneo and Romana, sending them pictures of the children every year until they graduated from high school. Romana said her husband kept them on his desk. When I visited Rome years later and called Romana, I learned that Dr. Cattaneo had passed away. He will be forever in my thoughts for giving me such good care and making my family possible.

Chapter 5

Bangkok, Thailand

After a long journey, we arrived in New York and took a flight to my mother's house in Pennsylvania so she could see the children. We stayed there for several days and then all drove to Washington DC in a green Chevrolet that Dave had bought. We settled down in a new house in Gainesville, Virginia. It was surrounded by a brick wall and built on a hill with lots of land.

But we didn't really settle down for long—only about ten months—before Dave eventually got orders for Bangkok, Thailand. We decided to rent our home while we were gone, so we contacted a real estate agent. She happened to collect teapots. We were away for several years, so I sent her many beautiful teapots. One teapot that I sent was an heirloom from China, and I wish I had it today.

Our flight to Bangkok would leave from California, so we decided to drive across the country. It was a great adventure. We encountered amazing snowstorms along the way, many which forced us to stay in hotels until the storms passed. Despite their ages, the children were wonderful—never a complaint or tantrum—and we made many stops. When we finally reached the west coast, we had the car shipped to Bangkok.

Finally, two weeks after leaving Washington, we arrived in Bangkok. It was desolate and poverty-stricken and seemed far worse than even Tehran. But regardless of the conditions, it was our new home.

Bangkok

We were assigned a poorly furnished room with two beds and a crib. We were brought some food, which made all of us sick. The walls and ceiling were covered with *chinchucks*, tiny lizards that seemed to be everywhere in Bangkok. At night, they would fall on us as we were trying to sleep.

One morning, our baby boy stood up in his crib, grabbed the side rail, and it collapsed. He fell on top of it and got a large bump on his head from the fall. We immediately took him to the hospital, where the doctor said he would be sore for a while but was fine. While I was in the waiting room, I struck up a conversation with a woman from the embassy, who happened to be there. I mentioned where we were staying and why my son was in the hospital. She suggested a new apartment building where there might be a vacancy on the third flood. I arranged for embassy transportation and went there immediately. Fortunately, the apartment was still available.

We moved in the same day. What a wonderful feeling it was to leave that horrible chinchuck-infested apartment! I found out later there were so few places available at the time that most embassy personnel were assigned similar accommodations. Back in the 1960s, there weren't all the hotels, malls, department stores, and restaurants there are in Bangkok today. Most people were living in huts.

The new studio apartment consisted of a large room with three beds, a small living area, a bathroom and a small kitchen. We were assigned two servants. They cleaned and did everything for us. The Thai people are very polite. They bow to you for every occasion and upon every meeting, which makes you feel like you're in another world—as does the music you hear playing in the streets and the beautiful temples you see everywhere. I could not wait to settle down and start enjoying and exploring the country.

Our servants carved large pineapples, which we purchased for ten cents each, into works of art. The bananas were also the largest I had ever seen; they cost one cent each. You could buy a centerpiece of orchids for only thirty cents. One day, the servant suggested we put our shoes outside the door, and they would be polished by morning. My little girl overheard this and, without our knowledge, collected all our shoes and put them outside the door. The next morning they had disappeared. The servant told her she should have put out only one pair. It was a good thing we still had the shoes on our feet.

Every day it seemed to get hotter. There was no air conditioning, and it was the worst heat we had ever encountered. Dave went off to the office, and it was up to me to find new living quarters. After consulting with embassy personnel, I located a beautiful house that was being built and would be ready for renting in a few weeks.

It seemed perfect. There were several Americans living nearby, so we'd have friends in the area. There was still time to choose colors for the walls, floors, and more. It had a living room, a kitchen, an upstairs and a downstairs bathroom, a circular balcony, and a covered terrace. The house included servants' quarters, so we hired a brother and sister as houseboy and maid. Like our previous servants, they kept bowing and smiling and seemed very nice.

The day we moved in, the houseboy and maid helped us open all the boxes, arrange the furniture, hang pictures, and even make the beds. Everything was perfect. We had a working television, and the embassy gave us a fan for the window in the living room. We were all so tired but happy to be there. The children loved playing on the terrace and enjoyed the house as much as we did.

But then the monsoon season arrived. Our teakwood floors started to expand and buckle. We called the owner, who decided to remedy the situation by having all the teakwood on the first floor removed and replaced with tile. She suggested we move to a hotel at her expense while the work was being done, which should take about a week. Despite the hassle of moving all our things to the second floor, we agreed. We had our houseboy stay there to protect against thievery.

A week passed and then another week. We thought we would never move back. Finally, the work was completed. We carried the furniture down from the second floor and re-hung all the pictures and drapes. There was so much to do. The houseboy and girl worked continually to help us get everything in order again. By the end of the day we decided to reward ourselves by going to an air-conditioned movie. The children were put to bed and the houseboy stayed downstairs—the usual procedure when we went out.

It was about 11:00 p.m. when we returned. The houseboy went to his quarters. I checked the children and went to bed. Later, I saw a light flicker outside and awakened Dave. He said it was probably just a reflection. But shortly afterward I heard my son scream, "Somebody!" He had just started to talk and that was all he could say. I ran to his room, but there was nobody there. He was so terrified I brought him back to bed with me, and soon we were all sound asleep.

The next morning I woke up, and even though I was still holding my baby, I didn't feel right. I woke Dave, who said he felt a bit groggy, but went downstairs. He didn't make it very far. In a calm voice, he said, "We have been robbed." I rushed to the stairs and saw that our first floor had been completely cleared out. The thieves had probably started stealing things from the second floor when our son screamed and scared them off.

When the police arrived, they told us the thieves had put us to sleep by burning a special leaf. They said most Americans are robbed at least once during their stay in the country. They suggested we visit the thieves' market and try to retrieve some of our things. (We actually found our television and a small window air conditioner there.) We later learned there had been seven thieves in our house; they called themselves "The White Horse Gang." After they robbed us, they took their truck across the street and robbed the neighbors.

As you can imagine, I didn't want to continue living in that house. We asked the owner if it was possible for us to break the contract. Under the circumstances, she agreed. We found a furnished apartment on the third floor of a three-story building and moved again. Embassy personnel lived there, so I thought it would be safer. The apartment had everything we needed. Our houseboy came with us, but his sister did not.

Everything was fine for a while. Marianne went to kindergarten at a Thai school, and my son stayed home with me. But one day the school called and said Marianne was having trouble breathing and that they did not have the authority to take her to a hospital. I immediately called Dave and told him I was picking up Marianne at the school and would be at the embassy dispensary shortly. When I took her to the hospital, the doctors checked her and she threw up. They suggested she stay overnight for observation. The next day she was a little better, so I brought her home. She eventually recovered, but we were never sure what had happened. Coincidentally, my son also became ill while we were in Bangkok. He had an attack of asthma and was in the hospital for a week.

It seemed like wherever we went in the city there was trouble. Even though the embassy advised Americans against driving because of the dangerous road conditions, I had driven all over the world and disregarded their suggestion. One day, I was driving slowly down the street not far from where we lived. Suddenly, a woman threw her child in front of my car. I didn't have time to stop and I ran over the boy. As if hitting him wasn't bad enough, I couldn't believe it when the mother picked him up, threw him in the back seat of my car, and ran away.

I remembered there was a Thai hospital nearby, so I drove there as fast as I could. The child was screaming, and I was frantic. But when I arrived, the gates were closed for siesta. I couldn't believe it! I laid on the horn until someone came out. I showed him the child, and he took him inside. Then I called the embassy. Dave, other attachés, a doctor, and an interpreter were there within minutes. Shortly thereafter, the mother of the child appeared and started demanding money. The doctor said the embassy and the insurance company would take care of everything and told us not to give her anything or she would continue this behavior. The insurance company took care of the bills, and the doctors took care of the child. I was thankful that the boy recovered and everything had turned out okay—or so I thought at the time.

To escape the hustle and bustle of the city, we often made the two-hour trip from Bangkok to Pattaya on the weekends. This town had wonderful beaches and a lovely resort with thatched huts right by the sea. Because there were no hotels at the time, that's where we stayed. The beaches also had other guests—hundreds of tiny monkeys that roamed everywhere. They were cute and harmless and were always begging for food. The monkeys were on the beaches and in the huts and would hide under towels or clothing and frighten you when you uncovered them. It was great fun, though, and the children loved them.

During our time in Bangkok, my father passed away. As soon as I received the telegram notifying me of his death, I made reservations to fly to the States. We decided Dave would stay in Bangkok with our son, and I would take Marianne with me. We left on commercial air with many flight changes and arrived two days later, the day of the funeral. It was winter, and I had to borrow warm clothes from my sister. After the funeral, we stayed one week and then flew back to Bangkok on Pan American Air. Three days later we touched down, ending a very long and tedious trip.

A few weeks later, the mother and relatives of the boy who I had hit with my car found out where we lived and started threatening us for money. The embassy stepped in again and told them if they did not stop they would go to jail. But it never stopped.

Another time I was returning to the apartment and, as I was starting up the stairs, I heard my son screaming. When I walked in the door, the houseboy and the servant girl had tied him to a chair and were pouring water on him and laughing. I immediately called the embassy, and Dave arrived within minutes. He grabbed the houseboy by his neck, threw him down the stairs, and fired both of them on the spot.

Again I insisted on moving to a safer place. There was a new high-rise building near the embassy, and because most of the residents were diplomats, we decided to move there. The British attaché and his wife were our neighbors. We hired another servant—a young girl who seemed fine. But she turned out to be no better than the rest. I fired her after just three days. The British attaché's wife admonished me for not giving her more of a chance and actually hired her the next day.

The following week, I was invited to high tea at this woman's apartment. All the ladies came beautifully dressed. Most were wives of diplomats living in the building. It was going to be a lovely party, but then we discovered that the servant girl had filled all the sugar bowls with salt. Our lovely tea turned out to be a disaster, and no amount of apology was adequate. Needless to say, the servant girl was fired again.

Occasionally, I took trips to Hong Kong. The attachés' plane (a C-47) could only accommodate ten people and, because children were not allowed, Dave would stay behind and take care of them. Hong Kong was fabulous because I could purchase so much for so little. I bought a beautifully carved teakwood bar for $80. It was four-feet tall with doors that opened all the way around and compartments for liquor and glasses. It still looks like new today. When it was delivered to the plane, the pilot didn't have room for it. We were overloaded with purchases! We had to leave it at the airport, and Dave picked it up on another visit.

Everything was finally going well in our new apartment. But then one day, once again, the relatives of the boy I had hit tracked us down. I was away from the apartment, and the children were with a new servant. She invited them in. One man lit a match and left it burning. Fortunately, I arrived shortly after they left, or there might have been a huge fire.

Dave and I had had enough. Our two years in Bangkok were almost over and he requested his next assignment. We received it with joy: Paris, France! The most wonderful place in the world! We started packing immediately.

Chapter 6

Paris, France

Even though we had visited Paris many times before, we were delighted to have the opportunity to live in this glorious city. I already spoke French, and Dave was eager to learn. When we arrived, we checked into a lovely hotel. The elevators smelled like a perfume factory. The room was quite nice, and it had a television set that you inserted coins into every ten minutes to watch. We turned it on to see President Kennedy in a parade. Little did we know what was about to happen.

The broadcast was in French. Suddenly, we heard shots. We could not believe what was happening. Our eyes were glued to the television, and Dave had to run down to the lobby to purchase more coins. The next day the French newspaper had all the details of the assassination. I saved that paper from 1963 for many years. Even though the newspaper yellowed, my memories of that day remained clear.

A week later we moved to a temporary apartment outside of Paris, and Dave flew to the French port of Le Havre to pick up the car we had shipped from Bangkok. We were also able to purchase another car from a person working at the embassy, who was leaving the country. Most of the people who lived in our apartment building were French. I met a French girl who was married to an American; she became one of my best friends during the five years we spent in Paris.

Not surprisingly, we had many visitors after moving to Paris. We'd usually take them to the Palace and gardens of Versailles, which were nearby our apartment. The Palace was largely decorated with marble and had many urns, busts, and a gilded balcony. The North Wing has a chapel, an opera, and picture galleries. The King's bedroom and the Queen's bedroom were especially magnificent. It takes all day to see the Palace and gardens of Versailles—the Chateau, the Grand Trianon, the Petit Trianon, and the Latona, Dragon, and Neptune fountains. Then there is the Hall of Mirrors and the Salon de Venus. The beautiful gardens have miles of paths that wind through groves, hedges, flowerbeds, pools of water, and more fountains. The Palace of Fontainebleau, which is also outside Paris, was another one of our favorite spots to take visitors.

The reason we were living outside Paris was because we were on a waiting list to get an American Embassy apartment in the city. While we waited, our children began classes at a French school. Marianne entered the second grade at a lovely convent school where only French was spoken. She was four-and-a-half years old, and she went there until she was almost six. Even at that age, French children go to school to learn, and there is little time for play. But the format worked, and Marianne was soon speaking French fluently as well as doing division and multiplication. David attended another school nearby, entering the first grade, and I either drove or walked both of them to school every day.

Finally, our name came up on the embassy list and we were assigned permanent quarters in Neuilly-sur-Seine, a suburb about four miles from the center of Paris. The apartment building was in a beautiful residential area not far from the embassy, which, incidentally, was located on the Champs-Elysées a few blocks from the Arc de Triomphe. A nearby Metro stop made it easy to travel all over the city. We unpacked and settled into our new, furnished home in one day. The apartment had a large living room, a dining room, three bedrooms, and two baths. We didn't have to worry about getting help, because each apartment was assigned two au pairs who did everything for us. Most of them were college students living in quarters in the complex. They were lovely girls and became like members of the family.

Because most of our neighbors worked at the embassy, we quickly made lots of friends. Maurice Chevalier, the French actor and singer, even lived close by. One day, we received an invitation for tea from a countess. I was delighted to be in her beautiful home. She was so gracious; *I* was the one who felt like royalty.

As we were welcomed into French society, our family also became more proficient in the language. We enrolled Marianne and David at the American School of Paris. Marianne was six, and the school informed us she was too advanced to be in the first grade with her brother, so they put her in second. While they were in school, I took morning French classes at the embassy.

I had plenty of opportunities to practice my French as I frequently traveled around the city. It was fascinating to take the Metro and shop in the beautiful department stores. I loved the Galeries Lafayette and Aux Trois Quartiers. I especially enjoyed the system they had for shopping. Each item you picked out was listed on a card. You carried nothing all day. You could lunch in their beautiful dining room and continue shopping in the afternoon. At the end of the day, you'd write a check for the full amount of your purchases or charge them. Your items would be all packed and ready or, if you wished, they could be delivered the next day.

Beyond shopping, there was so much to see and do in Paris. We visited the Louvre, the Eiffel Tower, the Opera House, Notre Dame Cathedral, and the Place de la Concorde, which is a spacious square with the finest architecture in the entire city. Through the embassy we were also able to get tickets for the theatre and most of the fashion shows. I attended these with several of my friends; we always wore hats and gloves to fit the mood of the event. We loved Christian Dior, a French fashion designer who is still famous today. One night, Dave and I saw a spectacular show at the famous Folies Bergère. The au pairs stayed in the apartment until we returned.

Another one of our favorite spots was the Place du Tertre in the heart of Montmartre, where many talented artists worked. It was breathtaking to watch them, and we purchased many of their paintings, some while they were still wet. The young men placed them in double wooden frames to dry.

Apart from the architecture and art, there was the food. Our favorite restaurant was La Grande Cascade. Whenever we had visitors from the States, we always made reservations there. We would arrive at 8:00 p.m. and were served the first course with a magnum of wine. There were many courses and each one came with a different magnum of wine. Of course, we didn't drink the whole bottle, only what we wanted. Finally, we were served a lovely dessert with a magnum of champagne. It was usually close to midnight when we left. All of our friends loved it. A politician and his wife from Washington visited us once, and we went to La Grande Cascade. After we drove them back to their hotel, the politician, despite his best efforts, walked straight into a glass window. His wife steered him to the door, and they both waved goodnight.

I had only one accident in Paris. When we first moved to the embassy apartments, I picked up several of my friends to go out for tea. Of course, we looked very smart wearing our hats and gloves. On the way, I had to drive from Champs-Elysées to the Arc de Triomphe. The cars were speeding in every direction. I slowed down to let one move in front of me, and he hit my fender. The driver was out of his car very quickly and said in an irritated voice that I should have speeded in front of him and then he wouldn't have hit my car. That was the day I learned that in Paris you must always speed faster than the next person. I never had another accident while living there.

While in Paris we also had the pleasure of hosting our parish priest from Virginia. His first request was to go to the Folies Bergère. We tried our best to discourage him, but he insisted. Dave called to purchase tickets but could only buy standing-room-only. Nonetheless, we were off to the Folies. In those days, priests wore their collars everywhere, and "standing room" was anywhere you could find a space, including in the aisles. At one point, we lost the priest. When we finally saw him, he was standing by the stage. Dave said, "I thought he wanted to see the Folies, not be in it." When the show was over, we went back to the car, and the priest met us there. He was elated, and said it was the best show he had ever seen.

Even though there was so much to do in Paris, we also traveled throughout France and Europe. One time we went to Lourdes, where thousands make pilgrimages to the blessed spring-water grotto every year in hopes of a miracle. We were amazed to see the throngs of people there, many of whom were maimed, blind, or disfigured. They all seemed to have so much faith. Hundreds and hundreds of people marched with lit candles, and we joined them with our children. We visited friends in the wine country of Bordeaux, where there were so many beautiful chateaux and gardens; we were overwhelmed by the acres of flowers and fruit trees. We also often visited Deauville, a spectacular beach resort associated with the rich and famous.

On these drives our children sat in the back seat, and we all played games, like naming the countries and their capitals. To this day, they remember the capitals of every country in Europe, Asia, and the Middle East.

We left Paris with sad hearts, but it was time to resume life on American soil. The sixteen years we spent living around the world was a wonderful and educational experience to be cherished forever. But now we would speak only one language. All the homes would look pretty much alike, and the neighbors would be friendly. It was 1969, and we were back to normal living in America.

Chapter 7

America, Part 2

When we arrived in the States after our long journey from France, we drove to our house in Virginia. We had entrusted a real estate agent to rent it while we were away. When we opened the door, we found a disaster. The last renters owned several large dogs, and the hardwood floors were stained beyond repair. All the doors were scratched. The kitchen appliances were so dirty they had to be replaced. It was not the beautiful home we had purchased seven years earlier. It was in such bad shape, we decided to sell it.

After some searching, we found a new development that we liked being built in the Fairfax area of Virginia. We bought the land and had a house built within the year. It was a beautiful colonial with three bedrooms, three baths, and a lovely staircase. It really was a dream home. Dave retired from Army Attaché and took a wonderful position with a corporation about ten miles from where we lived. The children were enrolled in school, and everything seemed so perfect. But then things began to take a turn for the worse with my husband.

Our new home in Virginia

Dave's position overseas as an attaché required him to attend many functions and parties. I believe, as a direct result of that, he had become an alcoholic. I thought once we settled down in the States things would be different. They were not. He continued to go out every night as he did in the past.

One Christmas Eve, Dave did not come home. I was so worried that something had happened to him. The next morning I received a telephone call from a hotel quite a distance away. They mentioned Dave's name and asked if I knew him. They said he had walked in from the cold in the early hours of the morning and asked for a room. He told them he had lost his car and didn't know where he was. I drove to the hotel to get him, and he really didn't remember what happened. I drove around the whole area looking for his car. It didn't show up until later in the week. I never said a word to him about his behavior.

Then it happened again. A few weeks later he went off to the bars, and he did not come home. When he showed up the next day, he packed his clothes and moved in with a young girl he had picked up the previous night. The last thing Dave said to me before he left was that he guessed he was never a family man. I was so upset that I filed for divorce that very day.

When the divorce was almost final, he called, crying into the phone. He told me that his girlfriend had thrown him out. He had no money and no job. He wanted to come home. But I said no. It was tough for me to take action like this against my own husband, especially when he was in this state, but I stayed strong. I knew our relationship could not—would not—continue.

It was difficult for me to have to care for the children, manage the house, and work all day—but my family managed to survive with me as the primary caretaker and breadwinner. My son didn't take the divorce as hard as my daughter, who had trouble accepting she would not see her father again. I still remember her saying, "Why did you let my sweet daddy leave?" She was less than ten years old, and the concept of divorce was foreign to her.

Although Dave was required to pay child support, I wanted nothing from him. And he had nothing to do with the children. I was happy to be free of him. Eventually, I sold the heavily mortgaged house and moved into a small apartment. I started working for the Pentagon as a secretary, and it took every cent I earned to send the children to private schools.

Eventually, both David and Marianne graduated from Bishop O'Connell High School in Arlington, Virginia, and went on to attend the University of North Carolina. I retired from my job at the Pentagon and moved to Florida. Then they both decided to transfer to the University of Florida, from which they both graduated. It was never easy for me financially or physically, but I managed to pay the bills and do everything I could for them.

My children both made wonderful lives for themselves. David accepted a job as an electrical engineer in Rhode Island and married a few years later. The following year, Marianne married a medical doctor. They had made it, and I had helped them. They were on their own.

My mother died in 1980 at age eighty-three, leaving me with an inheritance. For the first time in my life, I was free of worries and responsibilities. It was time for me to go on with my life, so I decided to travel again. During my time overseas with the Air Attaché I had studied seven languages. Now, it was time to test my memory.

Chapter 8

North America

Over the course of the next thirty years, I traveled the world. I visited countless countries—not all in one big trip, but in segments. I saw the sadness of some of the poorest cities of the world, the glitz of some of the richest, and the hope of every city in between. Each trip brought many wonderful people into my circle of friends, including a few celebrities. Though I largely traveled alone, my friends made me feel as if I never was. Along the way I also learned much about myself, both as a traveler and as a person on this great, vast, wondrous planet.

It all began in the still-untouched splendor of the Alaskan wilderness—the Russian Orthodox churches of Juneau, the breathtaking scenic drives through Haines, the great collection of totem poles of Sitka, the waterfalls of Skagway, and the bustling fishing industries of the port cities of Seward, Kodiak Island, Dutch Harbor, and Ketchikan, the salmon capital of the world and home to the Tongass National Forest, which stretches more than sixteen million acres across southeast Alaska.

In one of the greatest presentations of nature I've ever witnessed, I watched the tidewater glacier—great ice formations that shaped Earth into what it is today—break off into Glacier Bay. The sun gradually melts the ice and great blocks of the glacier. Then, pieces break loose with a piercing screech and go crashing into the water. I saw Mt. McKinley, the highest mountain in North America. And everywhere I saw signs saying "Beware of Bears." Luckily, despite all my adventures in Alaska, I've never seen a bear.

I also traveled throughout Canada, a vast country with a landscape as rich and as different as its people. I spent time enjoying the pleasant weather, colorful parks, and friendly folk of the royal city of Victoria. I treated myself in a queen-like fashion at the Empress Hotel, where one sunny afternoon I indulged in an array of sweets at high tea. I could only look, however, at Craigdarroch Castle, which looms high above the city, so beautiful that you can't help but stand in admiration. I wandered the fifty-five acres of Butchart Gardens. Each garden has a unique style: sunken, Japanese, rose, Italian, and Mediterranean.

In Vancouver, Canada, I met more friendly people and saw more beautiful gardens. I walked the elaborate Queen Elizabeth Park and the Nitobe Memorial Garden. As if all that natural beauty wasn't enough, I also witnessed the incredible thousand acres of scenic drives and beaches within Stanley Park. I understand why Vancouver is known as the Jewel of the Pacific. Finally, I traveled across the country to Halifax, Nova Scotia, the second largest harbor in the world after Sydney, Australia. This year-round ice-free port has a bustling downtown, and every day at noon you can hear an antique cannon boom from Citadel Hill.

With my tour of Alaska and Canada complete, I decided I would venture to warmer waters. It was time for the beautiful beaches of America's fiftieth state, Hawaii. The surf surrounding Honolulu on the island of Oahu is supposed to be some of the world's most treacherous. I chose to enjoy it from afar instead of on a surfboard. From the Nu'uanu Pali Lookout, I enjoyed breathtaking views. If you are thirsty, you cannot leave Honolulu without indulging in their famous Mai Tai, preferably enjoyed while strolling through the International Market Place and the Ala Moana Center. Both are joys for shopping. Oahu has a rich wartime history as well. The U.S. Arizona Memorial at Pearl Harbor is the final resting place for our brave Americans, as is National Memorial Cemetery.

From Oahu, I visited Lahaina on the island of Maui. Many artists are drawn here by the island's natural beauty, and their works are on display in the town's many galleries. To experience the island's natural history, you can view the famous Banyon Tree. This 60-foot tall tree was planted in 1873. Or you can take The Sugar Cane Express, an old-time steam train that travels six miles through the island. If you're lucky, you may even see a talking parrot or two.

We often forget about Alaska and Hawaii when we think of the United States of America, yet these two states are among some of our most stunning.

Chapter 9

Central America, the Caribbean, and South America

Although my journeys throughout North America were vastly different and fascinating in their own ways, they were familiar to me. Everyone spoke English, so I had no problem communicating with the locals. The cultures were largely American. Each city was accustomed to tourists. For a change of pace, and with a real sense for adventure, it was time to head south.

My exploration of Central America began in Mexico, where I explored many of the port cities. There was the scenic resort of Acapulco, a paradise of blue water and white sandy beaches, where cliff divers raised their arms overhead and bulleted into the sea more than 120 feet below. The feat is best enjoyed from the terrace of La Perla, a restaurant at the Hotel El Mirador. Acapulco is known as one of the world's greatest vacation playgrounds.

Then there was Puerto Vallarta, a resort town where the people were as colorful as the landscape. At the Mercado Municipal, the central market, you can buy pottery, masks, art, clothing, and more. The city is also home to some of the world's most exquisite yachts and beautiful beaches. So beautiful, in fact, that the famous actress Elizabeth Taylor and actor Richard Burton had a home there, which is now the Liz and Dick Museum.

In Mexico, I also visited the gorgeous beaches and movie-like vistas of Cozumel, Huatulco, Progreso and Cabo San Lucas. In Central America, I went to Puerto Quetzal, Guatemala. and saw the country's famous oversized bananas. I made several stops in Costa Rica as well, exploring the coffee plantations and rain forests of Puerto Limon and, of course, the retail "jungles" of Puntarenas. Apart from Costa Rica, I also visited Ecuador, a tiny country that still has a lively community. There is much to buy there, including handwoven rugs, guitars, and embroidered cloths. The famous Panama hat is also available for sale here, but from what I remember they were quite expensive.

Because much of my traveling was done via cruise ship, I spent a lot of time in the Caribbean. There was exquisite shopping for perfumes, fashions, watches, jewelry, electronics, leather goods, and many other items on Saint-Martin, an island that's divided 60/40 between France and the Netherlands. The Dutch influence carried to Curaçao as well, an island known as the Amsterdam of the Caribbean, with almost as many windmills as there are Italians silks, cameras, jewelry, and the famous Curaçao liquor available for purchase.

I experienced the luxury of St. Barts, the diver's paradise of Grand Turk, the incredible shopping of St. Thomas, the history of St. Croix, and the overwhelming number of beaches in Antigua—365, one for every day of the year. In Antigua, the major road is the scenic Fig Tree Drive, which can take you to Fig Tree Hill, with its farmlands of bananas, mangos, and coconut groves. Antigua also has amazing designer shops, boutiques, diamonds, watches and jewelry. Martinique, one of the largest islands in the Caribbean, smells wonderful. There are banana plantations, pineapple fields, and many lovely gardens. Because everyone speaks French here, if it weren't for the weather you might feel like you actually were in France. There are French designer clothes for sale and many perfumes.

I stopped in the Cayman Islands, known for their burgeoning business district and a popular post office called "Hell" from which you can send your friends postcards. I saw the mountainous islands of Tortola—which had many shops selling arts, crafts, spices, and wine—and the expensive beach homes of Barbados. In Barbados, I traveled around the island's bustling capital, Bridgetown, and then went north to the Platinum Coast, with its miles of sandy beaches and resorts.

I even explored Marigot Bay, St. Lucia, where Rex Harrison's *Dr. Dolittle* and Sophia Loren's *Fire Power* were filmed, as well as the Caribbean scenes of *Superman*. And there was beautiful Aruba, an island of beaches that's sunny year round. The highest point, Mount Jamanota, looks over all of Aruba, and the gorgeous Wilhelmina Park has tropical gardens right on the waterfront.

I also traveled through the grand marvel that is the Panama Canal, a journey that takes about nine hours to complete by ship. I met the small natives of the San Blas Islands surrounding Panama, then continued south to Ecuador (fabulous handmade rugs) and on to Lima, Peru, where I watched children play in the famous Plaza de Armas. Apparently jaguars lurk in the thick jungles of Peru. They're black and spotted and endangered—and I'm glad I never ran into one.

Off the coast of Chile on Easter Island I saw the massive moai. Some of these ancient statues, carved from volcanic stone, stand more than forty feet tall and weigh seventy tons. There are more than one thousand moai on the small island, all gazing toward the sea—and they're just about the only thing on the island as well.

Statutes, Easter Island

South America continued to amaze me with both its natural beauty and its architecture. In no place did these two worlds coexist more beautifully than in Valparaiso, Chile. This sprawling town clings to the hills of its landscape; each hill is like an individual city, with twisted streets and railways scaling the high elevations like elevators. Santiago is similar in its proximity to steep foothills, but much more modern than Valparaiso, with efficient railways and even ski resorts. I also witnessed the magnificent cathedral and town hall located in Montevideo, Uruguay, where I could almost feel the history. Buenos Aires, Argentina, showcased the beautiful contrast of old and new, too. The city is filled with colonial architecture, so much so that it's often called "The Paris of South America." I cannot agree more, having Paris so close to my heart. The Colon Theater compares to the Paris Opèra, and Palermo Park has lovely lakes and statues set in beautiful gardens.

Lastly, I visited the gorgeous country of Brazil. My first stop was Rio de Janeiro, one of the world's most beautiful ports. Standing high on top of Corcovado Mountain is the famous statue of Christ the Redeemer. The twin peaks, Corcovado and Sugar Loaf Mountain, are accessible by cable car, with fabulous views along the way. Copacabana Beach, where the women go topless and the men hang over the rails to watch them, is worth the visit to Rio alone. There's also the annual Carnival, which draws an amazing crowd of people to the weeklong spectacle.

The rest of Brazil has unique wonders as well. There's Salvador da Bahia, Brazil's first capital, which has ornate churches, lovely squares, and beautiful marketplaces. Convento de São Francisco is one of the most gorgeous churches I've ever seen, even in Europe. There's also Fortaleza, which is home to a major fashion show, and Florianopolis, south of Rio, with its endless supply of unspoiled beaches. And there was Recife, the Venice of Brazil, with its magnificent architecture.

Traveling throughout South American sparked within me a sense of adventure. There were so many beautiful places in the world to see, so much beautiful architecture to marvel, and so many more stores left to shop. It was amazing to visit each country and see the different cultures. Even the tiny islands had their own traditions. As I explored South America, I couldn't help but think to myself what else was out at sea, what other cultures awaited. Then I realized I knew my next destination.

Chapter 10

The South Pacific

You would think I'd had enough of enjoying skies without clouds, soaking up the splendor of untouched beaches, and shopping at some of the most exclusive boutiques in the world—but really, can one ever tire of that? The next leg of my world travels brought me again below the equator, to the myriad islands of the South Pacific, each one a gem in the seemingly endless stretch of crystal blue sea.

Aboard a ship, I jumped from island to island, taking in the unique locale of each for a day and then hopping to the next. Though my memories of the destinations tend to blend together, I remember a few high points from each island.

Bora Bora, located northwest of Tahiti, was my favorite. The people were fun loving and carefree. The island's shops contain black pearls, exquisite shells, and mother-of-pearl jewelry. They also sell real grass skirts and *pareus*, colorful garments that can be used for almost anything: sarongs, cover-ups, skirts, or dresses.

The best beach in Bora Bora is the Matura Beach. Paul Gauguin, famous for his modern art, lived here.

I also loved French Polynesia, from the small, unspoiled island of Moorea to the coffee plantations of Papeete to the vineyards of Rangiroa. In Rarotonga, I traveled the island's lone road, exploring the shops, museums, and a library along the way. I saw Raiatea and its tiny town of Uturoa. The country is famous for its fine beaches and yachts arriving from all parts of the world.

I traveled to St. Helena, a very small and remote island with abundant palm trees, ferns, pomegranate, and citrus trees. St. Helena is most famous for the fact that it was the island Napoleon was exiled and confined to until his death. He was buried in St. Helena until twenty-five years later when his body was exhumed and returned to France for burial.

There was also the island of Pitcairn, the smallest and most isolated of the South Pacific islands, sitting in the middle of the ocean yet teeming with life. The rock formations of Pitcairn are beautiful, as are the jungles. There are many books published and films made about the Bounty, a famous ship that sank off the coast of the island.

The last leg of my tour of the South Pacific brought me to Lautoka, the second largest city in Fiji. It has a rich sugar cane production system but is otherwise sleepy and peaceful. I also visited Apia on Samoa, an island of inspiration, where Gary Cooper's film, *Return to Paradise* was filmed, and Somerset Maugham's *Rain* also has roots. Finally, to complete my trip of the South Pacific, I explored Tonga, a grouping of more than 170 islands, and its capital city of Nuku'alofa. The Talamahu Market in Tonga has handicrafts, *tapa* cloth (a meticulously woven fabric), and carvings. Not too far from Nuku'alofa is Stonehenge, a massive and mysterious stone structure that's part of the ancient Tonga capital.

You would think that the islands in the South Pacific would be all the same. You'd think the people would look similar, talk similarly, and sell the same goods. But I was surprised to find that this was not the case. Each island had its own personality, sense of cultural pride, fashion, language, and means of making a living. Although most of the islands looked like tropical paradises, once I looked deeper, there was much more to be found. Each was unique and offered its own adventure. With my journey to the Edens of the world complete, I was starting to become eager for the bustle of bigger cities.

Chapter 11

Australia and New Zealand

I'll never forget the day I sailed into Sydney. The horizon was just starting to brighten as the cruise ship slowly made its way through the harbor. The famous architectural "shells" of the Sydney Opera House, which is right on the waterfront, began reflecting the changing colors of the sunrise. Along with Rio, Cape Town, and Hong Kong, it is one of the most beautiful sail-ins in the world.

The Opera House isn't just a masterpiece from the outside. It contains a number of halls, theaters, studios, and other venues that are used for symphonies, opera, ballet, drama, cinema, and just about every event imaginable. I attended a performance and climbed each and every step leading up to the main entrance. Years later when I returned to the Opera House, I found that, thankfully, there is now an elevator.

Beyond Sydney, Australia is a land of contrasts. Melbourne's streets are tree-lined and proper with miles of well-organized parkland, but not far offshore is Phillip Island, where you can watch the nightly mayhem as thousands of Little Penguins totter home at sunset. There's the grand Parliament House of historic Brisbane, but then farther north there's the natural wonder of the world's largest living structure, the Great Barrier Reef, a short catamaran ride from the city of Cairns. There's Perth, way out there in Western Australia, and the vast stretch of desolate outback that lies in the middle of the continent. Then there are the islands that circle the country—the plethora of birds and butterflies on Thursday's Island, the sand and surf of Hayman Island (where former president Bill Clinton once waved to us), and the sailboats and yachts of the Whitsunday Islands.

During my time down under, I also had the pleasure of exploring nearby New Zealand, a boomerang-shaped series of large and small islands off the southeast coast of Australia. My first stop was Auckland, known as the "City of Sails," because it claims to have more yachts than any other city. The climate is as pleasant as the population, which is comprised of Asians, Europeans, and the native Maori. Auckland is also a wonderful place to shop, filled with boutiques and designer stores selling sheepskins, wool garments, and jade ornaments.

Wellington—New Zealand's windy city—has narrow streets and cliff-hanging houses, plus cable cars to carry you up the mountainous landscape. I visited Tauranga, on the country's north island coast, the site of Hobbitown, where the movie Lord of the Rings was filmed. The city of Dunedin had one of New Zealand's loveliest landscapes, dotted with parks and churches, and imbued with a Scottish heritage. I also spent time in Christchurch, the ultimate English city outside of England. One of its most beautiful attractions is the Mona Vale Homestead. I also recommend taking the TranzAlpine train across the Canterbury Plains. It's one of the world's most scenic rail journeys.

Another part of New Zealand that I enjoyed greatly was Milford Sound. It took an entire day for our ship to sail up into the Sound and back, and the landscape was spectacular. We passed by waterfalls and snowcaps, and saw lots of wildlife.

Once, I even traveled to the chilly continent of Antarctica, but it was so cold I couldn't even write down what I experienced.

During my exploration of Australia and New Zealand, I found myself growing nostalgic. Both countries seemed to have a strong European influence, and I started thinking back to the time I had spent in Europe. Back then, I went sightseeing, but I never felt like I was fully able to see everything I wanted due to either my work or family responsibilities. But now, a free woman, I could set my own agenda.

Chapter 12

United Kingdom, Scandinavia, Europe, and More

I had spent a great deal of time in remote parts of the world—untouched wilderness, pristine beaches, and desolate backcountry. Exploring these areas was relaxing and enjoyable, yet part of me also wanted to reconnect with the city life I once knew so well from my time with the embassy. So I went back to the Old World.

My journey began in London. Big Ben, Westminster Abbey, Trafalgar Square, the Nationally Gallery, Buckingham Palace, St. Paul's Cathedral—I visited them all. I went to Guernsey, the beautiful Channel Island off the coast, where I spent an enjoyable afternoon in one of the pubs with friends. The ring of the church bell in Saint Peter Port would rustle the people every morning from their small houses, which seemed stacked atop each other like matchboxes. The port town of Fowey in south Cornwall was another favorite of mine. The rugged coastline in these parts actually harbors the remains of circular prehistoric stone houses.

After England, I traveled to Dublin and Waterford, Ireland. The latter is known for its crystal and its famous clock tower. During my travels, I met and became friends with Fred Astaire's daughter, Ava, and her husband, Richard McKenzie, who lived in a castle in Ireland. They were the nicest and most charming couple I've ever had the pleasure of knowing. To this day, I treasure their friendship. I even visited Scotland, namely the port of Lerwick on the Shetland Islands.

My next stop was Paris, which I consider one of the most beautiful places in the world. It was my first time back to the city since I had moved away so many years ago, and it was just as exciting as I remembered it. I visited many of the places I visited when I was living there—Notre Dame, Eiffel Tower, Latin Quarter, Champs-Elysées, Louvre, Galeries Lafayette—and enjoyed them even more.

From Paris I went to the world-famous French Riviera, where the countryside meets the sea. I spent time in Cannes and Marseilles. The latter, which is often overlooked by travelers to this area, is the oldest city in France and has some beautiful architecture, notably the Basilica Notre-Dame de la Garde with its lovely mosaics. The Côte d'Azur in Provence and its capital, Aix, is the City of a Thousand Fountains. The Cathedral of the Holy Savior has gorgeous Gothic architecture and majestic carved doors. It truly is a beautiful site worth exploring.

I couldn't resist taking a side trip to the tiny country of Monaco. It is known as the gem of the Mediterranean, and it does sparkle. The beautiful beaches are always crowded with bronzed bodies, and the harbor is filled with fantastic yachts. At night the Monte Carlo Casino comes alive with its gilded ceilings, crystal chandeliers, and elegant, well-dressed clientele. There's an important Grand Prix in Monaco, too. It's the world's *raciest* car race. People wear designer-everything and are there to be seen.

I concluded my tour of France in Bordeaux, with its fashionable designer boutiques along Cours Georges Clemenceau and Cours de l'Intendance. Of course, Bordeaux is also known for its wine. There are more than three thousand caves and chateaux within a short distance of the city.

From France, I set off for Norway, a surprising country with cities as beautiful as its untouched landscape. The bustling towns of Tromsø, the capital of northern Norway, Oslo, the capital of Norway proper, and Bergen, the capital of Fiordland, all have interesting museums, locals, and vistas. The ports of Svartisen and Flaam are especially pristine, surrounded by massive mountains, waterfalls, and glacial lakes. The views are spectacular.

In Scandinavia, I also visited the birthplace of children's author Hans Christian Andersen in Odense, Denmark. I saw the royal jewels at the Livrustkammaren Museum in Stockholm, Sweden. And I bought some elegant glassware in Helsinki, Finland.

Though I had lived in Rome years ago, I never had the opportunity to fully explore Italy, which was the next stop on my world tour. I was finally able to spend time at the Coliseum, the Forum, St. Peter's Basilica, and the Pantheon. Outside of Naples, I visited the ruins of Pompeii, one of the most famous excavation sites in the world, and the Isle of Capri, where I saw the Blue

Grotto. I also drove the winding Amalfi coast, with its dizzying views. In Venice, the dreamlike romance capital of the world, I navigated the streets of water to shop for exquisite Venetian glass, elegant tablecloths, leather wallets, and fine briefcases. In Genova, I witnessed the breathtaking architecture and collections of the Galleria di Palazzo Bianco (White Palace) and Rosso (Red Palace). In Catania, Sicily, I saw Mount Etna, the largest active volcano in Europe—a volcano I once visited and climbed when I was living in Rome.

Italy is a rich country in many ways. It's rich in the literal sense, as evidenced by the people of Porto Cervo, an exclusive seaside resort on the island of Sardinia where everyone wears designer clothes and eyewear of the highest standards. It's rich in the culinary sense, as evidenced by the town of Portovenere with its hills of vineyards and olive groves. It's rich in culture, as seen in Portofino, which movie stars and royalty frequent. And it's rich in history, which I saw in Florence, with its Piazza del Duomo, Piazza di San Giovanni, and the Baptistery.

My voyage throughout Europe was almost complete, but I still had a few destinations left to explore, the first of which was Spain. My survey began in the beautiful city of Barcelona, known for being alive with activity day and night. I loved the bustle and spent my time exploring the Cathedral de la Sagrada Fam'lia, the Picasso Museum, and Tibidabo Mountain, from which you can see the entire city.

After Barcelona, I stopped in Vigo, one of the rainiest and greenest towns in Spain, with lush mountain slopes, raging rivers, and gorgeous flowers. I traveled to Cádiz, an ancient city in the

Iberian Peninsula filled with great architecture. I tried my best to cover the many galleries in the Guggenheim Museum in Bilbao. Lastly, I visited the regal beaches of Málaga on the famous Costa del Sol (Coast of the Sun) and even took a side trip to the Rock of Gibraltar, which was—as it's notorious for—covered in tourist-loving monkeys.

From Spain I went to Lisbon, the capital of Portugal. The city is filled with beautiful monuments, statues, museums, and parks. The Monument to the Discoveries is the most stunning of them all. This giant structure juts out into the Tagus River, and in the distance you can see Europe's longest suspension bridge, named after Vasco da Gama. While I was in Portugal, I also visited Oporto, the city that produces the distinctive port wine, as well as the island of Madeira, where you can take a wicker-basket sled ride down a winding road. It's scary, but thrilling.

Greece was another country where I had once lived that filled me with nostalgia when I returned. I saw images of gods and goddesses carved in marble, painted on canvas, and etched in stone. In Corfu, Greece's Emerald Isle, I strolled the twisted streets to the Palace of Saint Michael and Saint George. Beyond its architecture, Corfu's shops offer exquisite leather goods, woven baskets, and their renowned crystallized fruit. I also explored Crete and the charming neighborhoods of Santorini, which are connected by cable car.

There are so many others places that I visited I almost can't remember them all. In Germany, there was Berlin, Frankfurt, Wiesbaden, and Warnemunde. In Croatia, there was Dubrovnik and Split, one of Europe's sunniest cities. The Split Cathedral has a collection of religious art known as the Treasury that is truly a sight to behold. Dubrovnik is a jewel of the Mediterranean, a walled city on the Adriatic Sea along Croatia's Dalmatian Coast. Mountains set the backdrop to an antique city, and the popular resort town is the perfect climate for lemons, oranges, grapes, and myriad flowers. Then there was Amsterdam in Holland, with its countless bridges, row homes, and bicycles in every direction I turned. I also enjoyed the excellent weather of the Canary Islands and its Mt. Teide National Park, which gives a spectacular view of the island's rock formations and volcanoes. The botanical gardens are home to more than four thousand types of flora and fauna. It is, after all, the place where the yellow bird found its name.

I also visited Iceland, and even St. Petersburg, Russia, which at the time was run down and sorely in need of reconstruction.

It felt good to return to some of the cities where I had once lived, as well as explore the neighboring areas. I could spend years in Europe, but I knew there was more of the world to see. My next adventure was to be completely different than any before.

Chapter 13

Asia

My reintroduction to Asia after many years came when I visited Kuala Lumpur, Malaysia. I was immediately struck by the city's architecture. One of the most impressive sights is the Railway Station, a combination of spirals, cupolas, and towers. Another impressive sight is the National Mosque, which is one of Southeast Asia's largest. It's adorned with towering minarets, surrounded by reflective waters, and it can hold eight thousand people. Sri Maha Mariamman is the city's most ornate Hindu temple. Inside is the famous silver chariot that's used in the annual Thaipusam festival.

Next, it was back to Bangkok. Since my departure nearly fifty years before, it had been transformed into a modern city with fine hotels, department stores, and high rises. Although the streets are jammed with cars, many people still get around in small rickshaw-like vehicles called *tuk-tuks* and on boats in the river canals or *klongs*. When I lived here, I used to buy twenty-five stunning orchids for twenty-five cents, but they're nowhere near that price now. Bangkok, too, has magnificent architecture. Picture a 150-foot-long, fifty-foot high reclining gold Buddha, and you will begin to understand the tributes the Thai people build to their religion.

Outside of Thailand's hectic capital, the country has many relaxing vacation spots, like Ko Samui Island, known as Thailand's playground. There you can watch monkeys scamper up and down coconut trees or ride an elephant to the Na Muang Waterfall. Phuket, another island, also has many lavish resorts and pristine beaches.

After Thailand, I traveled to Vietnam. I first stopped in the busy city of Ho Chi Minh, formerly known as Saigon. The main thing I remember about it was the chaos of the traffic. Thousands of bicycles, scooters, and pedicabs were each carrying not only passengers, but also animals and every imaginable possession. It was madness just trying to cross the street. Fortunately, I was able to escape it, if only for a while, when I lunched at the famous Rex Hotel and then slipped into a few small shops offering great buys at extremely low prices. Although the workmanship isn't as high as in Hong Kong, you can still buy beautiful material that can be made into dresses, suits, and drapes.

Away from the bustle of Ho Chi Minh is Vietnam's natural wonder, Ha Long Bay.

The many islands, grottos, and unusual limestone formations were created by relentless waves and winds over millions of years. And, to top it off, there are coral reefs, flooded forests, and tropical forests with thousands of animals and plants.

Almost as amazing is the Cham Museum in Da Nang (Chan May port). It houses three hundred sandstone and terra cotta sculptures and other important artifacts. Nearby are the Marble Mountains. Each of the mountains is named after a different element: metal, water, wood, fire, and earth. They are laced with staircases, caves, and tunnels that you can spend days exploring. Since I was so close, I also took a special trip to Angkor Wat in Cambodia. It's a Hindu temple complex that has incredibly ornate and exotic architecture.

After Vietnam and Cambodia, there was Singapore, which I still believe is one of the most beautiful cities in the world. It's immaculate. Importing and selling chewing gum (except brands considered to have health benefits like Nicorette) is illegal and punishable with stiff fines and even prison terms—you won't find any stuck under tables. There's also fabulous shopping in Singapore, and you can refresh yourself with an original Singapore Sling at the Raffles Hotel Long Bar afterward. They even encourage you to throw the shells from the free peanuts on the floor.

Every city, no matter how beautiful, has a nearby place to escape to, and Sentosa Island is Singapore's. It's a magical fairyland filled with beautiful flowers, trees, lights, and beaches. There's even a monorail now that takes you there. Dinner at one of the Sentosa Island hotel restaurants is an experience you will never forget.

Next, I was on to an even bigger adventure: China. First, I experienced Beijing, the country's capital and the center of the Chinese universe. I had lunch in the Grand Hotel, walked the walled palaces of The Forbidden City, and witnessed the splendor of the Hall of Supreme Harmony, which is one of the greatest architectural feats in human history. I stood on Tiananmen Square and visited the Great Hall of the People, where China's National Assembly meets. Not too many Chinese understood or spoke English when I was there; in fact, I can't recall carrying on a conversation with anyone. When you visit the department stores, you are on your own. Ask someone to help you locate an item and you just get a blank stare.

Hong Kong is different. I had visited there many times when I lived in Bangkok, and it provided some of the best shopping of my life. Ask someone for something there and they'll retrieve it for you. You could buy anything—silks, cashmere, jade, and more—at such reasonable prices. There is the morning market, the day market, and the night market. Today, the prices are much higher, of course, but you can still find anything you want. Hong Kong also has some of the world's finest hotels, including the Peninsula, Mandarin, Shangri-La, and Regent. All have tailors who will custom fit you for clothing and deliver it in days. I had dinner at the Peninsula several times with friends, and it was always fabulous.

Friends and I also visited the private Aberdeen Marina Club for lunch, wine and, believe it or not, fortune telling. A little bird would pick a card and give it to the fortune-teller, who would read your future. Unfortunately, "newfound wealth" wasn't in the cards for me when I later took the short hydrofoil ride to Macau, the popular gambling center.

After Hong Kong, there was Taipei, Taiwan, where I enjoyed the Chiang Kai-Shek Memorial Hall, with its marble towers, gardens, and ponds, all spread across more than sixty acres. Then there was Shanghai, the real "city that never sleeps." Bicycles were everywhere, because they're still the fastest way to move around the city. To relax and get some exercise, people do Tai Chi in the parks in the morning. One of Shanghai's most important temples is the Jade Buddha Temple. It has two statues of Buddha that are carved from rare white Burmese jade.

Continuing northward, I also stopped in Seoul, South Korea. Besides seeing the many royal palaces, I found my shopper's paradise at Itaewon, a special tourist area with thousands of stores and restaurants. Chongo, the downtown area, has many modern skyscrapers and high-rise apartment buildings. There are numerous movie theaters, restaurants, and department stores. A cable car will take you to the grand Seoul Tower and the Korea House.

Then it was on to Japan, of which I have many vivid and happy memories. Tokyo, the capital, was very expensive. Coffee in the hotels was about five dollars a cup, and dinners were extremely costly. I did enjoy the Kobe beef several times while I was there, and what they say is true: It is the best beef in the world. The Japanese people are very friendly, always smiling, and most of them speak English. In just about every shop I went into, they understood me.

Kyoto, Japan

I saw Yokohama, a bustling trading harbor. There's an area of the city called a "bund," which is known for its booming commercial enterprises. The Landmark Tower is the tallest building, and it has one of the world's fastest elevators. When you reach the 69th floor, there is an observatory with a spectacular view. Beyond the buzz of the city, there are also many parks, including Kamon-yama and its beautiful display of cherry blossoms.

Okinawa is the most developed island in Japan's southern archipelago. It has sunny skies, sandy beaches, and warm water. Okinawa also has a year-round temperature of about 75ºF. Also, there's an arcade of shops, department stores, boutiques, and restaurants. You can buy pottery, jewelry, and fabrics.

In Osaka, I had the pleasure of witnessing a traditional Japanese tea ceremony. The city is also a paradise for gourmands and a place of commercial importance. It's known as the "ancient water capital" and has many bridges and waterways as well. To get to Kyoto, a city of two thousand temples and shrines, I took the famous Bullet Train. At 131 mph, the trip took just fifteen minutes. I toured Nagasaki and the nearby Peace Park Museum, where you can wander through the statues, plaques, and monuments. And I traveled to Hiroshima, where I saw the massive, crimson Torii gates and Itsukushima Shinto Shrine. I stood at the gateway to the 12,300-foot high peak of Mt. Fuji in the city of Shizuoka. I explored the underground shopping malls of Nagoya. Lastly, I saw the white sands of Micro Beach in Saipan, an area that's renowned for swimming and snorkeling.

On separate trips, I also journeyed throughout India. I toured the luxurious Taj Mahal Palace Hotel in Mumbai and one evening attended a dinner for one hundred guests. There is amazing shopping in this city. The Zaveria Bazaar is the place to buy gold and diamonds. The Crawford Market has handicraft items, spices, antiques, carpets, leather goods, and almost anything else you could possibly want. Cottage Industries is a large shopping area behind the Taj Mahal Hotel where you can buy handicrafts from every part of the world.

Beyond Mumbai, there were the churches and temples of Cochin, India. There was Chennai, the "Hollywood of South India," where hundreds of films are shot each year. There was Goa, where the weather is always warm, and the beaches are always beautiful. I even had the pleasure of visiting the Maldives, a set of islands off the coast of India, where shallow blue waters brush up against white sand beaches, and colorful tropical fish race between the waves.

I also saw Myanmar, the former Burma, a country of much contrast. There are hundreds of shops where you can purchase silver, jewelry, designer clothes, and handicrafts, but the people are so poor. The Shwedagon Pagoda, a spectacular golden monument, towers above the poverty of Rangoon city.

I made several stops in Indonesia, but Bali was my favorite. It's one of the word's most exotic, historical, and magical places. There are many popular resorts and beaches here, as well as many adventures you can take, including exploring dark forests that house thousands of monkeys.

I was amazed by the diversity of Asia, from its architecture to its religions to its merchandise. There was a beauty in each country and a beauty to each people, who manage to live a more relaxed lifestyle than Americans despite all the bustle of their burgeoning cities. But even though I was often exhausted from shuffling among these crowds all day, I never grew tired of traveling. There was still so much of the world left to see.

Chapter 14

Africa

My visit to the erstwhile Dark Continent was like no other on my journey. I had lived in and visited many places during my time in government service, but I had never experienced this far and distant land. Each time I went to a new country in Africa, I was taken by surprise.

Cape Town, South Africa, was the most sophisticated, commercial African city I visited. The British influence is still present, so strong in fact, that every day at noon the Signal Hill cannon booms, and a changing of the guard takes place. The shopping in Cape Town was fantastic. One day I went shopping with a friend, Bob. We walked miles to find the right shop in which to buy large wooden animals. I think I bought half the store by the time we had to leave. Bob offered to carry most of the bags. We walked a long way on uneven and unpaved streets, and by the time we reached our destination he was exhausted. I was also loaded down and felt just as bad. He jokingly told our friends that he would never volunteer to go shopping with me again. Today I have just two of the wooden animals left, but Bob and I are still friends.

Cape Town also has outstanding beauty salons. You could go to one and have everything done—a haircut, styling, manicure, pedicure, massage, facial, and more. I'd sit there staring out along the shoreline wondering where in the world I was. Could this really be Africa?

Kenya provided my first real taste of Africa—the Africa I had seen in books and movies and what I had always imagined it would be like. I was fortunate to participate in three safaris. My favorite was in Tsavo West National Park, where I saw elephants, baboons, giraffes, hippos, and an incredible array of wildlife. In keeping with the flavor of the bush, Kenyan markets sells things you can't get most places, like spears, skins, and even animal teeth.

Safari, Kenya

Off the coast of Kenya sits Lamu Island, an area that was undiscovered by tourists when I traveled there. At the time, it had nine mosques, two cars, and no taxis. Donkeys were the only form of transportation—and four thousand of them lived on the island. There was even a donkey hospital.

Not far away is another interesting island: Zanzibar, off the coast of Tanzania. It's a large producer of cloves, cinnamon, pepper, and ginger, all of which I sampled.

Farther off Africa's east coast are the Seychelles Islands. Victoria, on Mahe Island, is one of the world's smallest capital cities, actually having more beaches (fifty-eight) than square miles (fifty-six). There are tea, vanilla, and cinnamon plantations, as well as art galleries, museums, open-air markets, and a 120-foot-tall coconut tree.

I also explored the west coast of Africa. My multilingual ability was humbled during my visit to Walvis Bay, Namibia, where the residents speak more than a dozen languages. My friends and I drove mini-cars across the sand dunes outside of town. By the end of the ride we were covered with sand from head to toe, but we all had smiles on our faces. There was also the quaint but beautiful Bom Bom Island Resort, with its pristine beaches and high palm trees.

Bom Bom Island

Abidjan, Ivory Coast, was a booming city with high-rise office towers, hotels, and boutiques. The Hotel Ivoire Intercontinental was the premier West African hotel at the time, with a bowling alley, cinema, art shops, and even ice-skating rinks. In neighboring Ghana, I toured museums, the House of Parliament, St. George's Cathedral, and the flower market. I also visited one of the tiniest African cities and countries: Banjul, Gambia. The nation had more than 560 species of birds at the time I was there, but hardly any people, it seemed.

Dakar, Senegal, was a thriving center of West African commerce. I toured the President's Mansion, which is surrounded by lavish gardens and several impressive-looking embassies. It is also situated near the Place de Soweto Monument, an area where vendors showcase carvings, antiques, and musical instruments.

In Casablanca, Morocco, I wound my way to the flower-filled central market and the gorgeous United Nations Square, with its fountain that illuminates the city at night. In Marrakech, I saw the fortune-tellers, street musicians, and dancers that the city is famous for, all gathered in the square. It was like experiencing the movie *Casablanca* in real-time. All I needed was the unforgettable song, "As Time Goes By" playing in the background—or, better yet, Humphrey Bogart on my arm.

In Gabes, Tunisia, I shopped the Berber Market, which sells everything, including spices, dried fruits, and jewelry. In Matmata, a mountainous city on the slopes of the Dunbar uplands, houses are carved into the earth for protection from the blazing heat. It is also where portions of the legendary *Star Wars* movies were filmed.

Overall, seeing Africa made me appreciate what I have much more. It's a continent of haves and have-nots, where material goods are sought after by some and considered unnecessary to others. It helped put the other countries I visited, with their grand sights and opulent lifestyles, into perspective.

Chapter 15

The Middle East

Our journey around the world is nearly complete, my friends. The last leg of the trip finds us in the Middle East, where there is much sand, but also much fun.

Although Istanbul is technically considered to be part of Europe, the rest of Turkey is in the Middle East. Everywhere you look around the city there's stunning architecture, including palaces, domed cathedrals, bridges, and mosques. There's also a fantastic *souk* (market) that's so big you can literally lose yourself in it. I also visited the Turkish city of Kusadasi. It's a resort town, with many streets of shops selling gold and beautiful jewelry. There are market places, the grand Library of Celsus, the Temple of Hardrian, the elaborate Trojan Fountain, and the majestic Arcadian Way, once paved in marble and lined with towering columns. It was a wonderful place to spend an afternoon.

Although I'd been there once before, one can never experience enough of Egypt. I stood at the base of the Great Pyramid of Giza and at the feet of the Sphinx. I walked the Museum of Egyptian Antiquities in Cairo and tried my best to view all 136,000 exhibits. The Tutankhamun Gallery alone has 1,700 magnificent objects that were retrieved from King Tut's tomb. I also visited his burial place in the Valley of the Kings and the exotic black sand dune beaches of Port Safaga.

Cairo, Egypt

Pyramids, Cairo

I witnessed the boom of Dubai while I was in the Middle East. The city is full of high rises, fabulous hotels, conference centers, luxury apartments, as well as such over-the-top attractions as an indoor ski slope and a set of manmade islands replicating countries of the world. Prosperity was everywhere. I was so impressed that I visited a number of times over the years. The people are well educated, prosperous, and polite. It is the city of gold—literally. There are shops selling gold everywhere. That's contributed to the area's nickname, the Pricey Coast.

The people of Oman were friendly, too. Muscat, Oman, is a center of history and architecture. There are many museums and galleries around the historic harbor that underline the importance of these seas over the centuries. Salalah is Oman's second city and an important part of the country's Dhofar region. North of Salalah is one of the three frankincense-growing areas. Although it used to be an important product for trade (right up there with gold and myrrh), it's now just mostly a novelty item sold to tourists.

The highlight of any Middle East trip, of course, is Jerusalem and Israel. I visited all the famous religious sites there, plus Bethlehem, Nazareth, the Sea of Galilee, and Zippori.

A close second, though, was Jordan, a country that both surprised and impressed me. Petra, the Lost City of Stone, carved thousands of years ago from the surrounding cliffs (and lately featured in an *Indiana Jones* movie) was simply amazing. Don't visit this part of the world without making time to see that.

Although I saw great riches in the Middle East, I was continually struck by the sheer amount of emptiness in the region. Despite the fact that I had traveled the world, that I had explored what I thought to be every nook and cranny, there were still so many parts of the planet that are untouched by humanity. It made be realize how small the human race really is—and myself as an individual, smaller still.

Chapter 16

The End of the Journey

As you can imagine, I accumulated quite a few items from all the countries I visited over the years. My three-bedroom condo was overstocked with rugs from Iran and China, beautiful paintings from France, Spain, and Thailand, chirping parakeets in a frame from Singapore, ceramic ducks from Burma, a wrought-iron-and-glass table (with chair) from Greece, wooden animals from Africa, antique wall clocks from France and England, Lladro figurines from Spain, Hummels from Germany, plus all sorts of china, crystal, ashtrays, books, and more. I even collected matches from hotels and restaurants, which I kept in a large glass bowl. One day a friend remarked that if lightning ever struck that bowl there would start a huge fire, and everything in my condo would be destroyed. The very next day I gave the matches away.

I met many celebrities, too, some of whom I now count among my circle of friends. I've shared my experiences with them, and they've shared their experiences with me. Through them and through their

stories I feel as if I know even more of the world. Looking back, I do not think my journey would have been as enjoyable without them.

Carol Channing

Shirley Jones & Husband

Tab Hunter

A few years ago, I decided to move to a one-bedroom condo, and I gave away most of my things. I had room for the basic furniture, one large rug, a few smaller carpets, several paintings, and only my most-prized possessions. Everything else went to friends and family. As I was sorting through it all, I often thought back to the places where I'd bought each item, the fun I had haggling for it, and the enjoyment everything had given me through the years.

All this traveling has contributed to an adventurous, wonderful, satisfying, grateful, and extremely full life. Now my life is almost over, and although I had so many great experiences, there is one that I somehow missed. In all my travels, I was never fortunate enough to find the love of my life—someone to share all these things with. I do not mean a love of convenience or for monetary reasons or even for the sake of the children. I mean a deep, enduring love that surpasses everything else in the world to become greater than life itself. Even though I've had a wonderful life, I think the most important thing one can accomplish is finding true love. I wasn't able to do it, but when a person does, she has conquered the world.